How To Discover And Break GENERATIONAL CURSES

50 Powerful Prayers To Destroy Evil Foundations

Efemena Aziakpono Anthony

Copyright © January 2020 by Efemena Aziakpono Anthony

All Rights Reserved.

No contents of this book should be reproduced in any way or by any means without obtaining written consent from the author or his representative.

Published By:

Better Life Media

Your Testimonies, Calls And Texts Are Welcomed

"Our fathers sinned and are no more but we bear their iniquities. Servants ruled over us; there is none to deliver us from their hand. We get our bread at the risk of our lives, because of the sword in the wilderness. Our skin is hot as an oven, because of the fever of famine. They ravished the women in Zion, The maidens in the cities of Judah. Priest was hung up by their hands, and elders were not respected. Young men ground at millstones; boys staggered under loads of wood. The elders have ceased gathering at the gate, and the young men from their music.

The joy of hearts as ceased; our dance has turned into mourning. The crown has fallen from our head. Woe to us for we have sinned! Because of this our heart is faint; Because of these things our eyes grow dim; Because of Mount Zion which is desolate, with foxes walking about on it." – (Lamentation 5:7-1)

Table Of Content

Chapter 1: Introduction 6

Chapter 2: Problems Of Evil Foundation 21

    Prayer Points 44

Chapter 3: How To Interrogate And Investigate Your Foundation 46

    Prayer Points 65

Chapter 4: How To Deal With Evil Foundation 66

    Prayer Points 96

Chapter 5: How To Prepare For Family Deliverance 97

    Prayer Points 105

Chapter 6: 21 Prayer Points To Undo The Evil Foundation 107

About The Book 114

About The Author 116

"Therefore thus says the Lord God: Behold, I lay in Zion a stone for a foundation, a tried stone, a precious corner stone, a sure foundation; Whoever believes will not act hastily." – (Isaiah 28:16)

Chapter 1: Introduction

"Our fathers sinned and are no more but we bear their iniquities." – (Lamentation 5:7)

This is the problem of evil foundation and most people are victims. They are wrongly suffering for an offence they did not commit but was committed by their fathers.

But they are running up and down seeking for a way out everywhere. It was the fathers that sinned but they, the children have inherited the anger with the consequences of their sins.

In Exodus twenty and verse number five the bible reveals that the children will pay for the sins of their fathers to the third and fourth generation of those who hate God because He is a jealous God.

"... For I, the Lord Your God, am a jealous God, visiting the iniquity of the fathers

upon the children to the third and fourth generation of those who hate Me." – (Exodus 20:5)

From Genesis to the book of Revelation and throughout the pages of the bible God has vowed never to share His glory with any other. No one ever touch His glory and go free whether in heaven, earth or earth below.

All over the world and from one generation to another there were and there are people who were and are crying not because they did anything wrong on their own but for the sins of the fathers.

Just as all of humanity inherited the sin and the consequences of the fall of Adam, even so most people have inherited the sins and consequences of their father's house.

Most problems of life are closely related and tied to one's foundation whether of birth or marriage. Name and call it family evil pattern or foundation problem, they both mean the same thing.

A careful study of the bible and the history of the families on the earth reveals and shows a certain pattern of life of victory and success or of woes and unexplainable tragedies and calamities that befall people from every age.

Some people may argue but the truth remains that while some have inherited a blessings, others had inherited a curse or an evil foundation.

The forefathers have committed evil against God by worshipping and serving other gods and living contrary to the word of God. They may have also done evil against their fellow men deserving of judgment and death and are gone and the children have to live with the consequences.

The scripture is clear if one does not repent and acknowledge the Lordship of Jesus, he or she will live and die a sinner and end up regrettably in the lake that burns with fire.

Evil foundation is the reason for most battle cry in this life even among believers.

There are many born again, spirit filled and tongue talking believers who are suffering the same thing their unbelieving fathers, uncles, brothers and sisters suffered and are still suffering. They are suffering the same pain, the same shame and affliction with their unbelieving brothers and sisters in their respective family.

The question then is; where is the testimony of the believer? What is the essence of the faith of our Lord Jesus?

Where and when is the promised rest? Is it only in heaven that a believer will find rest? Many questions, isn't it?

When and where a believer is going through what unbelievers are suffering, it may not necessarily be a problem of personal sin or trials of faith as some may easily and cheaply conclude. It may be that there are foundation problems demanding attention.

Foundation has a voice and that voice can and do cry for or against a people.

In the book of Proverb chapter thirteen and verses twenty two is one passage to watch.

"A good man leaves an inheritance to his children's children.

But the wealth o the sinner is stored up for the righteous."

What does it mean?

A good man will leave something good for his children's children. And a bad man will lose his riches to the children of the righteous. And what will be left for his children can at best be imagined.

The scripture further tells us that the blood of righteous Abel cried out to God. What was it crying for? Was it crying to bless or curse the elder brother who murdered him in cold blood?

No, it was crying for justice and vengeance. Wherever there is offence or a wrong, there will also be demand for justice.

And our God is a God of justice; there is no unrighteousness with Him forever. He is first just to Himself, to the devil and to man.

I hear people say God is all powerful and almighty. They reason that He should just bind the devil and cast him into the bottomless pit and prevent evil on the earth.

Some even cry, God you hate me. Why do you allow me to fall into these and that problem? It is very easy to shift and pass the blame. God is not a respecter of man or any creature for that matter. He is strictly bound by His word. He is a covenant keeping God and will do nothing apart from His word. He will never compromise his word and covenant.

Most people crying for help from one altar to another knew next to nothing about the foundation of their fathers left for them. And, you know something, ignorance is not cheap nor an excuse.

And again, not many people care about the foundation of their in-law's house.

At the time of marriage, it may not matter occur to them to check. But later after the marriage is consummated, and life is not what they plan for and expected they starting crying out and may be accusing everyone but foundation.

Most people building families and businesses around the world do not really care about foundation. All they care about is their ambition, not the plan of God.

Foundation is important if you really desire an enduring record of victory, success and breakthrough in life and career. It is foundation that carries a building and if that foundation be faulty, then you will have to be ready for the consequences, if not the worse.

What do you know about your father's house? How did they live their own lives? What about your in-laws or the family you married to or from? What do you know about their history?

For you to have a smooth and easy journey in life, marriage, business or ministry, you have a duty to make sure that the foundation you are building or walking on has what it take to sustain the type of life, building, career, or home you have in mind.

There are foundations and there are many foundations indeed. But there is only one sure and tested foundation. And you can only find it in Christ.

> *"Therefore thus says the Lord God: Behold, I lay in Zion a stone for a foundation, A tried stone, a precious corner stone, a sure foundation; Whoever believes will not act hastily." – (Isaiah 28:16)*

And again;

> *"For no other foundation can anyone lay than that which is laid, which is Jesus Christ." – (1 Corinthians 3:11)*

You see, from the very beginning of creation God has a purpose and a pattern of life for all His creatures. But the fall of Adam subverted the divine pattern and foundation for all mankind.

But the unchanging nature of God and His plan cannot be compromised.

I see men rise to the position of honor only to tumble from top to bottom, very young and promising young people lose their lives without any explanation for their premature death, whole family struggling with one crisis or another without any to explain. And these things happen all the time.

What could be responsible if not foundation?

If all your fathers had and left for you was evil foundation and your experience of life and family is that of a tale of one crisis after another, then that must be a call to investigate and interrogate your foundation.

There is no smoke without fire and effect without a cause.

If one is ignorant of his or her foundation of birth or marriage, that person may suffer long and many are suffering really.

Ignorant of law is not an excuse if one is held in court for an offence. You will be made to face the full wrath of the law.

"People do not despise a thief if he steals to satisfy himself when he is starving. Yet when he is found, he must restore sevenfold; he may have to give up all the substance of his house." – (Proverb 6:30, 31)

So even if you may not have chosen your parents or ancestors, you may suffer for their wrong or enjoy their goodwill if any.

Where you are born again, you must take the necessary steps required to free you from the backload of evil that were and are the direct result and consequences of the wickedness of your fathers or in-law's house.

In (Deuteronomy 18:9-14), God warned Israel not learned and follow the way of the gentiles because their manner and way of life was a direct opposite of the will of God for His people.

"When you come into the land which the Lord your God is giving you, you shall not learn to follow the abominations of those nations."

What was the custom of these people and why the strict warnings?

In verses ten to twelve of the same passage above, we see the record the things the gentile's do and practice that the Lord considered an abomination and they were the reason God was dispossessing them of their inheritance.

"There shall not be found among you anyone who makes his son or his daughter pass through the fire, or one

who practices witchcraft, or a soothsayer, or one who interprets omens, or a sorcerer, or one who conjures spells, or a medium, or a spirits, one who calls up the dead. For all who do these things are an abomination to the Lord, and because of these abominations the Lord your God drives them out before you.

You shall be blameless before the Lord your God.

For these nations which you will dispossess listened to soothsayers and diviners; but as for you, the Lord your God has not appointed such for you."

According to the scriptures, the portion of land Canaan occupied was richly blessed by God but they lost it to Israel because of their abominable manner of life.

City life and the wind of civilization blowing across the globe may not allow you to know some of the things that go on in your ancestral home or village. But if your ancestors or parents were involved and practiced any of the things the Lord considered an abomination in that passage of scripture, or you are not pleased with your experience of life, it means and may require you to investigate your foundation and prepare to undo or suffer its consequences.

If these things were considered an abomination then, there is no way and place in the scriptures that will accommodate them today and forever.

Human ritual or sacrifice, witchcraft, soothsaying, divination and the likes may be accepted norms and practice today. But that does not mean they are acceptable standards for living in the word of God.

This book is an answer to the cry of many who are going through difficulties that have no explanation. It is a wake-up call to many who are ignorant of the problem of evil foundation.

It is recommended to all who desire real changed in the circumstance of their lives.

It is also recommended to all who desire a solid foundation for an enduring breakthrough for themselves and the generation yet unborn.

Do you have a history of disappointment, stagnation, unfruitful labor and marriages, premature death, total abject poverty, undue delay in life? Is it a common occurrence among your people?

Investigate because they may not be unconnected with foundation problems.

My desire and prayer for you is that the Lord will help you to find an enduring solution and answers to your every challenge and question of life.

Read and pray the recommend prayer in this book and recommend to your friends and enemies alike.

Let it be my little contribution for your wellbeing by the power of the Holy Spirit. And by the grace of God I will hear your testimony in the name of Jesus.

Life will be much easier if we get our foundation right. And don't you ever forget foundation has a voice!

God bless.

Efemena Aziakpono Anthony

Chapter 2: Problems Of Evil Foundation

"Our fathers sinned and are no more, but we bear their iniquities." – (Lamentation 5:7)

This was a testimony of a people who were experiencing hardship and pain not for any fault of their own but for the sins of their fathers. And this was the situation with Israel for many years.

It was so bad that it became a proverb among the people of God at that time.

"What do you mean when you use this proverb concerning the land of Israel, saying: 'The fathers have eaten sour grapes, and the children's teeth are set on edge'?" – (Ezekiel 18:2)

These people were aware that the problems and difficulties they encountered and were living with was not any fault of their own. They could trace it to the sins of their fathers who were no more.

How did they come to know about these things?

They have a history that helps them to understand their problem. They were the privilege race upon the earth and had dealing with the creator.

They had teachers and prophets who guided them from one generation to another.

Yet they repeated the mistakes of the fathers again and again.

What is your history like? Does it point you to God or you are one of those who think it doesn't matter?

God had made man for His glory but that was till the fall of man. Adam could not keep the estate that was trusted to Him.

He committed a sin popularly known as original sin, a sin punishable by death and got everything on earth messed up.

And we, his offspring's have inherited his sin with all its consequences.

That is how all human problems began and lost touch with the almighty God the maker of heaven and earth.

And all flesh became children of the devil and idolatry and immorality became the order of the day.

Man was created to worship and serve his Maker but was cut off from his place in God because of sin.

To say that God hate idolatry and immorality is an understatement.

Any people given to the practice of idolatry and immorality forever become an abomination and enemy of God.

Before we talk about problems of evil foundation, it will make a lot of difference to consider the word foundation.

Now, what is foundation?

Foundation is the base upon which a house or building is standing. It is that unseen part of a building that holds and sustains a house in the good and bad times.

It refers to a set of laws, regulation, or principles of belief by which a people are raised and governed. It also refers to the norms, traditions, culture or a people's way of life.

Cultures and traditions differ from one family and nation to another across the world. While some are Christians, others are either Moslems or traditionalist.

In this book and chapter, we are considering evil foundation and the problems associated with it.

Whatever your foundation, it is the word of God alone that determines whether a foundation is good or evil, the result notwithstanding.

Evil foundation is a foundation of a people built on idolatry and immorality. It is a foundation laid and built apart from God.

> ***"Unless the Lord builds the house, they labor in who build it; unless the Lord guards the city, The watchman stays awake in vain." – (Psalm 127:1)***

Evil foundation also refers to a cursed foundation and people.

The curse may arise as a result of a breach of existing contract or covenants with the almighty God.

It could also be as a result of breach of covenants with an idol, a fellow man or evil family altar.

These evil altars are known to fight back when the prescribed sacrifices are not given to them as at when due.

The curse could also result from the wickedness of man against man.

A witch doctor could project evil against his or her so called enemy as Balak invited Ballam to do to Israel but for divine intervention.

"Now Balak the son of Zippor saw all that Israel had done to the Amorites.

And Moab was exceedingly afraid of the people because they were many, and Moab was sick with dread because of the children of Israel.

So Moab said to the elders of Midian, "Now this company will licks up the grass of the field." And Balak the son of Zippor was king of the Moabites at that time.

Then He sent to Ba'laam the son of Beor at Peth, which is near the River in the land of the sons of his people, to call him: look, a people have come from Egypt. See they cover the earth, and are settling next to me!

Therefore please come at once, curse this people for me, for they are too mighty for me. Perhaps I shall be able to defeat them and drive them out of the land, for I know that he whom you bless is blessed, and he whom you curse is cursed." – (Numbers 22:2-6)

A people may also suffer a curse because of the wickedness of their fathers.

Scriptures reveals that Canaan inherited and suffered a curse laid on his father by his grandfather for spying and mocking him while he was drunk and naked.

"And Noah began to be a farmer, and he planted a vineyard.

Then he drank of the wine and was drunk, and became uncovered in his tent.

And ham the father of Canaan, saw the nakedness of his father, and told his two brothers outside.

But Shem and Japheth took a garment, laid it on both their shoulders, and went backward and covered the nakedness of their father. Their faces were turned away, and they did not their father's nakedness.

So Noah awoke from his wine, and knew what his younger son had done to him. Then he said, Cursed be Canaan; A servant of servants he shall be to his brethren. And he said: Blessed be the Lord, the God of Shem, and may Canaan be his servant.

May God enlarge Japheth, And may he dwell in the tents of Shem; And may Canaan be his servant." - (Genesis 9:20-27)

The tribe of Reuben was almost wiped out of Israel but for Moses, the man of God. Reuben was cursed for sleeping with his father's wife.

> *"Reuben, you are my firstborn, my might and the beginning of my strength, the Excellency of dignity and the Excellency of power.*
>
> *Unstable as water, you shall not excel, because you went to your father's bed. Then you defiled it. He went up to my couch." – (Genesis 49:3, 4)*

And so beyond idolatry and immorality, evil foundation is a cursed foundation. It is a foundation of iniquity and gross evil and wickedness.

The wind of civilization blowing across the globe has so blinded most people that they knew next to nothing or carless about the foundation they came from and are building on.

If you were born and brought up in a family or community that worship idols and practice immorality, or is placed under a curse, even if you are born again, you are ignorantly sitting on a keg of gun powder.

The Canaanites lost their ancestral homes to Israel for their idolatrous and immoral lifestyles.

The cities of Sodom and Gomorrah were destroyed for the same reasons.

Israel the nation and people of God were not exempted from judgment whenever they learnt and practice idolatry with their neighbors.

One problem of idolatry and immoral lifestyle is that it makes one an abomination- enemy of God. It also opened a wide door for Satan to use and destroy you.

And if God is your enemy you can at best imagine what life will be like.

The sin of idolatry and immorality defiles the land and invokes strict judgment on a people and their land.

Read (Psalm 106) and you will find a detail account of the things that unbelievers or gentiles bring on themselves by idol worship and immoral life-style.

Idolatrous families suffer double curse and passed the same to their children's children yet unborn.

The idols they offend will fight them and the generation yet unborn and they stand no chance at all before the almighty God whom they flagrantly turn against.

There are several problems associated with a people that practice idolatry and immorality. If you care to check it out, you will notice high level of wickedness among them-witchcraft, human sacrifice, power tussle to mention just a few. Among them also, you observed poverty, backwardness, sicknesses and diseases of various type, premature death, rising and falling, delays in marriage and child birth, disappointment, violence and several other hardship.

There are many people roaming about the streets, some fasting and praying really hard, seeking and looking for a way out of these problems.

There are communities and nations too, which has not known development because of incessant bloodletting and wickedness by the fathers.

Of a truth, there are communities and families on the earth today that will not know and see any development until they accept Jesus.

It may never occur to them that the foundation of their lives was wrong from the very beginning.

For such people and nations, the gospel of Jesus is the only hope.

It is true,

"Therefore, if anyone is in Christ, he is a new creation; old things are passed away;

> ***behold, all things become new." - (2 Corinthians 5:17)***

The new birth is a reality, no doubt about it. But how will the old things acknowledge in the above passage passed away?

Jesus suffered and paid the penalty for sin for all mankind. That victory will never be yours till you enforced it in your life. You must own that victory by living the new life.

Even though you are born again and filled with the Holy Spirit the scriptures still tell us to work out our salvation with fear and trembling.

> ***"Therefore, my beloved, as you have always obeyed, not as in my presence only, but now much more in my absence, work out your salvation with fear and trembling." – (Philippians 2:12)***

When the Holy Spirit says to work out your salvation, it means and suggests that there are things you must attend to after you are born again.

A careful student of the bible will notice that after Gideon found mercy, God commanded him to go and destroy the evil altar of his father's house.

Daniel too, understood by books that Israel bondage in Babylon will last seventy years and after those years they will regain freedom.

But scripture reveals that Daniel the man of God went to God in prayer confessing and repenting of the wickedness of his father's house.

If you neglect and fail to repent and handle the evil foundation of your father's house in the way of the Lord, even though you are born again, you may speak all the tongue and quote all the scriptures I care, you may not make or see any progress in life.

Certainly, you will make it to heaven, no doubt about that but on this earth, you may barely survive.

This is one of the reasons most believers are struggling with almost everything in life.

Being born again does not exempt any one of us from the challenges of this life.

There are very faithful and committed Christians going through unimaginable suffering and difficulties.

Why?

Make no mistake about it, it might not necessarily be your fault or the trial of faith as most may assume and conclude.

Ignorance can make you suffer wrong and suffer long really.

Foundation has a voice and when it speaks, men must listen or respond.

The two foundations

In (Mathew 7:24-27), Jesus spoke on the two foundations.

"Therefore whoever hears these saying of Mine, and does them, I will liken him to a wise man who built his house on the rock:

And the rain descended, the floods came and the wind blew and beats on that house; and it did not fall, for it was founded on the rock.

But everyone who hears these sayings of Mine, and does not do them, will be like a foolish man who built his house on the sand:

And the rain descended, the floods came, the winds blew and beats on that house; and it fell. And great was its fall."

Considering that passage you will notice that one is built on the rock and the other, on a sandy soil. The one on the rock he described as a solid foundation and the other on the sandy soil as a faulty foundation.

The one who built his house on the rock He called a wise builder. The one on a sandy soil he referred to as a foolish man and builder.

One thing is common to both builder; they will face the same challenge or challenges.

In other words, every one of them will be subjected to the same test and one will survive the test and the other ruined.

Let me ask you, which of these two foundations will you prefer to build on?

Just a guess, no wise builder will ever want to build what will not last not to talk of what will be destroyed.

The bible has this to say, a wise or good man leaves inheritance for his children's children.

But what if all your father's left for you, were evil foundation of idolatry and immorality; unsettled family grievances and debts or curses and covenants; evil altars and shrines, what are you going to do?

Simply carry on just because you are born again?

A million times no.

As I said before, these things have a way of fighting back. Ignorance of law is not an excuse.

You must settle down and rise up in faith to interrogate and investigate your foundation to uncover the depth of idolatry and immorality they gave in to and take appropriate measure to address them in Christ.

If your family or city is cursed, you must labor in faith to break the curse.

Jesus said, every tree His father did not plant must be uprooted.

It is your responsibility to undo the wickedness of your father's house. The reason is so you will not suffer for their sins.

There are too many people going through unimaginable things they can't explain except they look into the foundation of their lives.

There is this family with a history of delayed marriage and outright childlessness.

One of the daughters found favor and got married to a man of God. After many years of prayer and fasting, she got deliverance and happens to be the only one that has given birth so far out several of them.

Upon investigation, it was discovered that their fathers were involved in a murder of one of the wives of the family simply because she was blessed with long life.

Because of her age, the family decided to force her death by burying her alive concluding that she must have been a witch and the one responsible for the suffering and death of younger ones in the family.

But before they could cover her up alive in the grave, she laid a weighty curse on the family that no woman in the family will ever get married and if they did, they will never give birth.

Women from this family even though some of them are born again, are going through this problem till date.

The sister that had a breakthrough among them did not keep quiet. She took steps to address her foundation before her breakthrough.

You cannot ignore foundation.

In (Mathew 22:23-32), is the story of a family in which

Seven brothers died without a child having been married to one woman.

"The same day the Sadducees, who say there is no resurrection, came to Him and asked Him,

Saying, "Teacher, Moses said that if a man dies, having no children, his brother shall marry his wife and rose up offspring for his brother.

Now there were seven brothers. The first died after he had married, and having no offspring, left his wife to his brother.

Likewise the second also, and the third, even to the seventh.

Last of all the woman died also...."

What was wrong with this family was not revealed but it was obvious all the brothers died of the same problem.

It is my prayer that what probably killed your fathers and brothers will not kill you.

For the purposes of emphasis, I will say it again that foundation has a voice and whenever it speaks something good or evil will definitely happen unless someone rises up to stop it.

Someone must rise up strong in the faith of the lord Jesus to stop the power of evil foundation in your life and family.

One other problem of evil foundation is that it has a way of repeating the same mistake with the same consequences.

If your father was a witch doctor the probability that one of the children will be a witch doctor is almost fifty to fifty, if not hundred percent.

The same thing too, if your fathers were warrior or warlords, renowned thieves or cultist, the tendency is always there for one of the children if not all of them to repeat the same error and bring more guilt and punishment on the family.

Put another way, it becomes a bloodline problem that may linger for decades or generation unless someone call the family to order in the lord.

Child of God, there are problems associated with evil and a cursed foundation.

But there is hope, I mean, there is hope for you in Christ if you will wake up from your slumber.

I will not close this chapter without a word of caution.

There is no smoke without fire. Something led your fathers to idol worship and something brought about the family curse.

Some of them were out genuinely looking for help or a way out of their troubles and ended up in the hand of the enemy of their life-the devil.

In trying to solve or find solution for one problem or the other they brought their children yet unborn into more trouble.

And today they are not around to explain what happened to their children who have become the heir of the trouble and problem they caused.

You too, must be very careful as you go about life seeking for solution and ways to make things happened otherwise your posterity will never forgive you.

I first heard it from Rev. Mike Murdock that one will be remembered for the problem he caused or the problem he solved. May you be ever remembered for the one you solved? May you never cause one more problem for the generation unborn? They already had enough.

Are you in a hurry to make it in life?

Remember, Abraham waited for twenty five years to have his Isaac. Our God is never late. If you keep faith with him, you too will testify.

Prayer Points

- Thank the Lord for the family of your birth and or marriage.
- Thank God for the salvation of your soul
- Pray that God will make you the Gideon of your father's house.
- Pray that God may give you light to better understand the foundation of your father's house.
- Pray that God may empower you to undo the evil of your father's house.
- Pray very well so that you will not repeat the mistakes of your fathers.

- Pray! O God expose the foundation of my father's house.
- Pray and receive grace to build on the sure and tested foundation revealed in scripture.

Chapter 3: How To Interrogate And Investigate Your Foundation

In the last chapter, our focus was on the problems associated with evil foundation.

In this chapter I want to show you what and what you must look out for in your foundation to determine and establish that your foundation is good or evil.

My purpose in doing this is to help you make a firm decision that will turn your life and situation around.

I believe you have suffered enough and it's your turn to break out and break forth of that evil foundation.

Now let's begin with this scripture.

"For we are God's fellow workers; you are God's field, you are God's building.

According to the grace of God which was given to me, as a wise master builder I have laid the

Foundation, and another builds it. But let each one take heed how he builds on it.

For no other foundation can anyone lay than that which is laid, which is Jesus Christ.

Now if anyone builds on this foundation with gold, silver, precious stones, wood, hay, straw,

Each one's work will become clear; for the day will declare it, because it will be revealed by fire; and the fire will test each one's work, of what sort it is.

For if anyone's work which he has built on it endures, he will receive a reward.

If anyone's work is burned, he will suffer loss; but he himself will be saved, yet by

so as through fire." – (1 Corinthians 3:9-15)

In Genesis chapter one and verse twenty six, the scriptures clearly stated that man was made in the image and likeness of the Almighty God and was given authority to subdue the earth.

From the very beginning of creation, God created man to partner and co-labor with Him upon the earth.

Even after the fall, the redemptive plan did not change the original plan of God concerning His man.

"For we are His workmanship, created in Christ Jesus for good works, which God prepared beforehand that we should walk in them" – (Ephesians 2:10)

God's eternal plan has always been for man to work with Him in the administration and development of the earth.

The scriptures reveal how Adam betrayed and subverted the original plan by yielding to the devil instead of God.

And so, as supposed co-workers and partner with God on the earth we cannot afford to build and develop our lives and the earth apart from Him.

Moses was warned to build according to the pattern that was shown to Him.

> ***"And see to it that you make them according to the pattern which was shown you on the mountain" – (Exodus 25:40)***

Beloved, God has a pattern, manner of life for all His creatures on the earth. Consider the serenity, the fellowship and the level of authority that man had and exercised in the garden before the fall. That was and is still the mind of God for all of man.

If you or your fathers did not build according to the original pattern given to Adam that Jesus came to restore, you must and should reconsider what you are building.

> *"For no other foundation can anyone lay than that which is laid, which is Jesus Christ." – (1 Corinthians 3:11)*

You see, you are not permitted to build whatever you like and choose. You must keep in mind that you are a man under authority and you are here to seek His glory at all times and in every situation good or bad.

Interrogate and investigate the foundation your father's laid down for you and be sure that you are standing on the right part to build your own life.

Do the same yourself and find out whether the pattern of life, work, marriage and family that you are building is according to His divine plan and purpose.

A wise builder will do this; subject his own work to scriptural test. It will save you from public embarrassment and eternal judgment.

Beloved, whatever the Lord has called you to build or do; you must be very careful how you go about it.

And the reason: your work will be tested for what sort it is.

"Therefore whoever hears these saying of mine, and does them, I will liken him to a wise man who built his house on the rock:

And the rain descended, the floods came, and the wind blew and beat on that house; and it did not fall, for it was founded on the rock. But everyone who hears these sayings of Mine, and does not do them, will be like a foolish man who built his house on the sand: and the rain descended, the flood came, and the winds blew and beat on that house; and it fell. And great was its fall."

According to this passage, the same thing will happen to both the wise and foolish builder. One will be destroyed the other will survived the trial.

In (1 Corinthians 3:9), the bible says,

"For we are God's fellow workers; you are God's field, you are God's building.

Jesus is saying to you and me, to be careful first of all because we are partner with Him, secondly because we are the field and the very building.

And so, be careful how you build or live your life. Every building will pass through the test.

And if anyone must build or live, he or she must build according to the plan of God. And that is the only way for your building to pass the test.

Beloved, why will anyone build what will not last?

Who will knowingly start a journey or business he knew will eventually fail?

But that is the irony of life. People don't really care how they build. That is the reason for so many collapsed buildings, marriages, families and businesses.

Where you lay and build on a faulty and weak foundation you should know what to expect. It is a matter of time and as my senior brother will always say, time will tell.

Now if you found any of the problems associated with evil and cursed foundation manifesting in your life or family, how will you go about it?

There is virtually nothing new under the sun. There are records to show you are not the first or only one going through things like that.

Therefore, interrogating and investigating your foundation is the ultimate reason this book is written and presented so you can find a way out of your predicament.

I will not forget in a hurry the testimony of a man of God who shared his experience with us on one of the mountain I ascended to seek the face of the Lord.

As at the time he was sharing with us, he was forty five years old and he was the oldest man in his father's house and family.

He told us no one ever crossed forty five years in his father's house and that his father, mother, brothers and sisters, uncle and aunties all died before they were forty five.

He said to us, as he was approaching that age, he became troubled knowing fully that it was his own turn to die.

Though, he did not tell us the cause of premature death in the family, he told us he resigned to faith and began to seek the face of God concerning the situation.

And that was how he crossed the line of premature death in his father's house.

I believe God for you right now and prophesy into your life that you are next to testify in the name of Jesus.

Few years ago, a sister joined our prayer fellowship.

One day she came and reported how every December, they were hosting burial ceremony of the husband's brothers one after the other.

As we sought the Lord in prayer it was revealed that the case was one of a land dispute.

While we were still praying a brother in-law died.

After the death of that brother, the sister took it upon herself to champion the cause of freedom for her husband and after that prayer; it's been almost three years now and there has not being another death in the family.

Beloved, you must interrogate and investigate your foundation to uncover the cause of prevalent calamities and determine the extent and depth of prayer to be carried out for your freedom.

If you observe that your brothers and sisters or father's house has the ugly experience of premature death, poverty and hardship, delayed marriages and child birth, a history of disappointment and evil cycle of sicknesses and diseases, or don't keep marriage or home, rising and falling or near miracle situation always; then stop and think of what to do.

There are a number of things to do to uncover and break part with the evil report of your father's house.

First of all, you must resolve it in your mind that you are going to pray and bring the situation under control.

Jesus made it clear that there is a need to pray and pray through in the gospel of Luke18 verses one.

"Then He spoke a parable to them, that men always ought to pray and not lose heart."

When there is a crisis situation, what most of men does is complain or quit.

But we all should know that complaining alone about a bad situation does not amount to a thing or bring change.

One must be ready to take steps to bring about the desired change. And one of those things to do to bring that change is persistence prayer of faith in the lord.

Secondly, why you are praying you must also seek godly counsel about your experience and situation. Discuss your observation and experiences with relevant authority over your life, may be your pastor or father in the faith.

Counseling is important that is the reason the bible says in the multitude of counsel there is safety. Seek godly counsel over your problems if any. A closed mouth is a closed destiny. Someone somewhere has a key to the solution of your problem.

Humble yourself to seek that godly help that will turn your life around.

Thirdly, compare notes with others in your environment- family to be sure it is or it is not a family problem. It is a family problem and connected to evil foundation if the same thing is happening to other members of your family repeatedly. May be it happens to your grandfather and then to your own father and now it is repeating in your own life, and you can see it going round in your father's house. That is the evidence you need to investigate and fight for freedom.

Based on your findings, carry out what I will call spiritual mapping on your family or father's house.

I have observed men go down when it was their turn to be honored and celebrated. I have seen and read of men disgraced out of office or position for no just cause. I have also observed men and women rise to the peak of their chosen career tumbled down in shame. There are reports and testimony of many who suddenly became stranded and stagnant in life after they got married or attain a particular age or height in life.

These things do happen and unless one attends to them, they may persist forever unabated.

Search the scriptures and you will find out the Lord has no plan to humiliate His creation.

I say this not to intimidate but to provoke you to do what you have to do scripturally to overcome and conquer evil foundation.

Why?

These things don't just happen. There is need to investigate and interrogate your foundation so you may know the reasons or causes of the problem and prevent a repeat of the same mistakes that led to them.

Based on your findings, you must probe further if there were known curses, acts of wickedness committed against others, altars and shrines of devoted idol worship and service, blood or human sacrifices, witchcraft and cultic practices, ancestral worship and calling up of the spirit of the dead and several other evil practices in the family.

Identify the altars and shrines by name and location. Identify the sacrifices offered to each altar, the laws guiding the different shrines and why.

In Israel, the tribe of Reuben was almost wiped out but for Moses the man of God.

What happened?

Reuben slept with his father's wife and on his death bed Jacob laid a curse on him.

"And Jacob called his sons and said, "Gather together, that I may tell you what shall befall you in the last days: Gather together and hear, you sons of Jacob, And listen to Israel your father.

Reuben, you are my firstborn, my might and the beginning of my strength, the

excellency of dignity and the excellency of power.

Unstable as water, you shall not excel. Because you went up to your father's bed; then you defiled it He went up to my couch." – (Genesis 49:1-4)

The tribe of Reuben paid for the sin of their father for years till Moses' intervention.

"Let Reuben live, and not die, nor let his men be few." – (Deuteronomy 33:6)

Moses the man of God was the one that interceded for the tribe of Reuben and break the curse that was against them.

The sins of your fathers against fellow men can be a burden on the family.

Investigate and interrogate the lifestyle of your fathers whether they were involved and guilty of such sin as murder and illegal and forceful possession of properties like house, human sacrifices, and shrines' priest and repent of these evils.

If your fathers were known strong men and warriors, you must trace the powers behind them and prayerfully undo the evil works.

Also find out whether your father or any of the fathers was a known cultist.

Interrogating and investigating your foundation is for the purpose of freeing yourself and family from the evil that evil family foundation represents and cause.

And so you will need to do a thorough investigation.

Be willing to ask who must know all relevant questions that will lead to ultimate deliverance and freedom for all or you in particular.

Find out the names of all the idols and their altars and the depth of sacrifices that were usually offered to them.

For some altars or shrine the blood of a cock is enough but not so with others. The level of sacrifice determines the level of wickedness of the spirit behind the evil altar. There were and are altars and shrines that were raised with human blood.

You must also find out what your family forbid and why. Some family will not eat certain animals and or crops. There is reason for everything under the sun.

Daniel found by books the number of years Israel will remain in exile in Babylon. May be he also discovered other things that led to their exile in Babylon.

You too, can find all the information you care about to effect or enforce your family deliverance.

You must summarize your findings to enable adequate planning for the warfare.

Interrogating and investigating your foundation also requires you to seek the face of God concerning all your findings to ascertain the accuracy of your findings and confirmed same by the Spirit of God.

If you call upon the Lord, he will show you things you know nothing about in your father's house and the reason for everything.

"Call to me, and I will answer you, and show you great and mighty things, which you do not know." – (Jeremiah 33:3)

God is true to His promises.

And so, take time to seek the face of God for direction and deeper understanding of the problems in your life and family. If you do, you will find the help only God can give.

Gideon was the man God used to defeat and deliver his own people from slavery and bondage to the Philistines.

It was not his strength and wisdom that delivered the land but God. God help Gideon and his people to gain freedom.

I can assure you God is ready and willing to give you help and usher you into a new realm of life where you will never know the Egyptians that your father's knew, dreaded and served.

Read the sixth chapter of Judges and you will notice that Gideon did not trust his skills and intelligence.

Of course, the arms of flesh will always fail and so, no use trying or attempting to rely on anyone of them.

Prayer Points

- Ask the Lord to oversee this project
- Ask the Lord to grant you the co-operation of everyone that you will need to accomplish this project.
- Pray for wisdom to confidently wage this war to a logical conclusion.
- Pray for divine protection and provision for this exercise.
- Ask the Lord to anoint you for this project.

Chapter 4: How To Deal With Evil Foundation

Before I proceed to discuss and address how you may handle the problem of your foundation, let's discuss something very important so we can better prepare to deal with it.

Somebody may say he or she has no business with the evil foundation of his or her father's house because he or she is born again. Honestly speaking, I once said so too.

But the big question is does it exempt one from suffering for the sins of his or her father's house?

Let me state it here that when God gave the ten commandment and other laws in the book of Exodus and chapter twenty, He did not give it to the gentiles but to Israel His covenant people.

A careful student of the scriptures will notice that any time Israel stray from the written code and its commandments, they suffer the same problem as the gentiles.

And so, when God said the children will suffer for the sins of their fathers to the third and fourth generation God was not addressing the gentiles. He was talking to His covenant people.

In (Ephesians 6:12) the scripture says,

"For we do not wrestle against flesh and blood, but against principalities, against powers, against the rulers of the darkness of this age, against spiritual hosts of wickedness in the heavenly places"

This passage was not written to unbelievers. Rather, it was written to warned believers against the activities of the evil powers of darkness.

Therefore being born again does not exempt you from the wiles of the devil. You must stand firm in faith to fight and win in the battles of life. And one of these battles is the battle of evil foundation.

The new birth put you in advantage position to undo and deal with the evil foundation of your father's house where they exist.

Read the bible and you will find out that often times the children of Israel were afflicted for the sins of their fathers.

*"**Hezekiah became king when he was twenty five years old, and he reigned twenty nine years in Jerusalem. His mother's name was Abijah the daughter of Zechariah.***

And he did what was right in the sight of the Lord, according to all that his father David had done.

In the first year of his reign, in the first month, he opened the doors of the house of the Lord and repaired them.

Then he brought in the priests and the Levites, and gathered them in the East square and said to them: Hear me,

Levites! Now sanctify the house of the Lord God of your fathers, and carry out the rubbish from the holy place.

For our fathers have trespassed and have done evil in the eyes of the Lord our God: they have forsaken Him, have turned their faces away from the dwelling place of the Lord, and turned their back on Him.

They have also shut the door of the vestibule, put out the lamps, and have not burned incense or offered burnt offerings in the holy place to the God of Israel.

Therefore, the wrath of the Lord fell upon Judah and Jerusalem, and He has given them up to trouble, to desolation, and to jeering, as you see with your eyes.

For indeed, because of this our fathers have fallen by the sword; and our sons, our daughters, and our wives are in captivity.

Now it is in my heart to make a covenant with the Lord God of Israel that his fierce wrath may turn away from us." – (2 Chronicles 29:1-10)

This passage is a story of the revival of King Hezekiah. It tells us the reasons for the troubles they went through and the steps the king took to turn away the anger of the Lord and bring deliverance to his people.

Yes, Hezekiah was in a very privilege position to undo the wickedness of the fathers.

The fathers has forsaken the Lord and turned away from the house of the Lord. They put off the lamp of the house of the Lord and stopped burning incense in the house of the lord and brought the wrath and judgment of God upon them.

Hezekiah gathered the Priest and Levites and commanded them to

Sanctify themselves for the service of the Lord

Sanctify the house of the Lord and clear the rubbish that was in the house of the Lord

Made up his mind and restore temple worship with all the daily sacrifices and offering.

Called and restored the priesthood and the Levites to their service in the house of the Lord.

When you read further, you will see how he called the people together to seek the mercies of God.

He was able to get the people back in favor with God.

In the case of Gideon, he was commanded to pull down the evil altar in his father's house and raised a new altar unto the God of Israel.

"Now it came to pass the same night that the Lord said to him, Take your father's young bull, the second bull of seven years old and tear down the altar of Baal that your father has, and cut down the wooden image that is beside it.

And build an altar to the Lord your God on top of this rock in the proper arrangement, and take the second bull and offer a burnt sacrifice with the wood of the image which you shall cut down." – (Judges 6:25, 26)

Beloved, you can't overlook the wickedness of your fathers and expect to blossom in this life. Even if God keep quiet over the matter, the idols and the evil altars will fight silly for recognition.

The reason some of us have to go over again and again one problem is because we are good in taking things for granted. We like to explain everything away.

There is no reason at all to intimidate you with the problems of evil foundation with their attendant consequences.

Oftentimes, those who raised the evil altar were not informed of the consequences that will follow in case of a breach of contract. Your father's intention at the time may just be to secure his heritage and family.

But according to the book of Lamentation, they brought idols to the family and sinned against God and are no more. The children are left alone to bear the consequences.

The idols are fighting and the children cannot get any help from God until these things are addressed in the faith of our lord Jesus.

Think about it, you are born again, spirit filled and speaking in tongues yet things are not right with you.

You may be very hard working but can only barely survive. What on earth could be the problem if not foundation?

There are many very faithful believers who are suffering and stranded in life and they are unable to explain the cause of their predicament.

Beloved, don't try to make light of these matters.

A particular woman in the gospel had serious health challenges and Jesus addressed her as the daughter of Abraham yet she was afflicted for eighteen years. It was her encounter with Jesus that brought about her deliverance.

The point is this, even though you are born again, grow your faith and pay attention and attend to your foundation. May God give you grace to know what to do to overcome the trouble of evil foundation.

In (Hosea 4:6), the bible has this to say,

> ***"My people are destroyed for lack of knowledge. Because you have rejected knowledge, I also will reject you from being priest for me. Because you have forgotten the law of your God, I also will forget your children."***

According to this scripture, it is not God and not Satan but ignorance that is the problem of most people.

They lack accurate knowledge of what to do about their problem. Even, when they are told they would put up very strong argument refusing to do the needful.

Friend, to enjoy deliverance and overcome the challenges of this life, you need information.

Jesus said and I quote,

"Then Jesus said to those Jews who believed in Him, if you abide in my word, you are My disciples indeed. And you shall know the truth, and the truth shall make you free." – (John 8:31, 32)

Truth, knowledge of truth is key to your freedom. It is knowledge that determines your placement in life. And if you are not informed you will be deformed. This information is for your perusal. Use it to advantage.

Now let's begin to consider some of the steps you must take to undo the evil foundation of your father's house and gain freedom for yourself and your unborn children.

Remember that by evil foundation is referred a cursed foundation. By extension, they constitute evil altars, covenants and curses resulting from the atrocities committed by the fathers against God and fellow man.

Any foundation that is not built upon the principles of God's word is a cursed foundation.

Let's take a look at the confession of Israel in their trying times.

"Praise the Lord!

Oh, give thanks to the Lord, for He is good!

For his mercy endures forever.

Who can utter the mighty acts of the Lord?

Who can declare all His praise?

Blessed are those who keep justice.

And he who does righteousness at all times!

Remember me, O Lord, with the favor You have toward Your people.

Oh, visit me with Your salvation,

That I may see the benefit of Your chosen ones,

That I may rejoice in the gladness of Your nation,

That I may glory with Your inheritance.

We have sinned with our fathers, we have committed iniquity,

We have done wickedly.

Our fathers in Egypt did not understand your wonders;

They did not remember the multitude of your mercies, but rebelled by the sea_ the Red Sea.

Nevertheless He saved them for His name's, sake

That He might make His mighty power known.

He rebuked the Red Sea also, and it dried up;

So He led them through the depths, as through the wilderness.

He saved them from the hand of him whom hated them, and redeemed them from the hand of the enemy.

The waters covered their enemies; there was not one of them left.

Then they believed His words; the sang His praise.

They soon forgot His works; they did not wait for His counsel, but lusted exceedingly in the wilderness, and tested God in the desert.

And He gave them their request, but sent leanness into their soul.

When they envied Moses in the camp, and Aaron the saints of the Lord.

The earth opened up and swallowed Dathan, and covered the faction of Abiram.

a fire was kindled in their company; the flame burn up the wicked.

They made a calf in Horeb, and worship the molded image.

Thus they changed their glory,

Into the image of an ox that eats glass.

They forgot God their Savior,

Who had done great things in Egypt.

Wondrous works in the land of Ham, awesome things by the Red Sea.

Therefore He said that He would destroy them,

Had not Moses His chosen one stood before Him in the breach, to turn away His Wrath, lest He destroy them.

Then they despised the pleasant land; they did not believe His word.

But complained in their tents, and did not heed the voice of the Lord.

therefore He raised up His hand in oath against them, to overthrow them in the wilderness,

To overthrow their descendants among the nations, and to scatter them in the lands.

The joined themselves also to Baal of Peor, and ate sacrifices made to the dead..

Thus they provoked Him to anger with their deeds, and the plague broke out among them.

Then Phinehas stood up and intervened, and the plague was stopped.

And that was accounted to him for righteousness to all generations forevermore.

they angered also at the waters of strife so that it went ill with Moses on account of them;

Because they rebelled against His Spirit, so that he spoke rashly with his lips.

They did not destroy the peoples,

Concerning whom the Lord had commanded them, but mingled with the Gentiles and learned their works;

They served their idols, which became a snare to them

They even sacrificed their sons and their daughters to demons

And shed innocent blood, the blood of their sons and daughters, whom they sacrificed to the idols of Canaan; and the land was polluted, with blood.

Thus they were defiled by their own works,

And played the Harlot by their own deeds.

Therefore the wrath of the Lord was kindle against His people, so that He abhorred His own inheritance.

And He gave them into the hand of the Gentiles, and those who hated them ruled over them.

Their enemy also oppressed them, and they were brought into subjection under their hand.

Many times He delivered them; but they rebelled in their counsel, and were brought low for their iniquity.

Nevertheless He regarded their affliction when He heard their cry;

And for their sake He remembered His covenant, and relented according to the multitude of His mercies.

He also made them to be pitied by all those who carried them away captive." – **(Psalm 106:1-46)**

Read through this chapter of the book of Psalm and you will discover how the people brought trouble into their own lives and family.

By their evil examples they set up an evil pattern for the generation unborn and brought the wrath of God upon their unborn children again and again.

According to Psalm11:3, what shall the righteous do if the foundations are being destroyed?

Watch helplessly and do nothing? No, a million times no.

The righteous must rise up to the challenge of re building the foundations. That is what people like Ezra, Nehemiah, Elijah and Daniel did. And that is what is expected of you.

In (Daniel 9) you will find a pattern of what is expected of any one that will champion the course of restoration and deliverance for his people.

What did Daniel do differently?

He took time to find out the reasons for everything they were going through and did not pretend as most people will like to do. He did not become the devil advocate but uncovered the wickedness of his fathers.

Daniel confessed the sins of his fathers and repented of the same. He did not stand in defense of the evil they committed nor perpetuate them.

Daniel and many others, who deemed it wise labor to return the people to God, called the people to repentance and rededicate the nation or families to God.

They cleaned up the holy place and restore worship of the almighty God.

They renewed their covenants with the almighty God and did not pretend about it.

They pleaded for the mercies of God and turn away the wrath and anger of the Lord.

Repent and seek the mercies of God for your father's house. Take a stand of faith; ask forgiveness for the atrocities they have committed. And you know what! The Lord will graciously forgive and pardon every sin that brought shame and sorrow to the family. The curse will be broken or lifted and the family will be free from all the consequences and effect of the household wickedness.

"He who covers his sins will not prosper. But whoever confesses and forsakes them will have mercy." – (Proverb 28:13)

In most families there is nothing left of the evil altar, I mean physical and visible evidence of it. When I visited my father's house for the same purpose there was nothing on ground to point us to any evil altar.

The evil tree has been removed and all the ceremony around the evil altar stopped but spiritually speaking the altar was in place. The demon behind the altar was still hanging around and disturbing the good and the peace of the family.

When the lord opened my eyes to see, I saw a mighty altar or shrine in the compound. I saw the glory of the family held bound by the evil altar.

I saw in the spirit how I went in with axe and anointing oil in the dream to pull down the evil altars.

God may be showing you pictures of this nature but may be you don't still understand really.

You see, the absence or destruction of a physical or visible altar does not represent the true state of affairs.

In my own case and before the lord intervened in my life, one of my uncle went ahead of me to remove the evil tree in my father's house. But in the spiritual realm the Spirit of God was still pointing me to the tree.

The point is this; don't allow the absence or destruction of the physical altar to deceive you to believe that the work has been done. You must address this matter spiritually.

Yes, remove the physical altar, but also address and cast out the spirit behind the altar.

Until that happens you can't conclude your liberation.

In (Judges 6) Gideon was commanded to pull down the shrine and destroy their tokens and he did.

At day break the people gathered to fight for the idol. Hear what the father of Gideon said to them,

"But Joash said to all who stood against him, would you plead for Baal? Would you save him? Let the one who plead for him be put to death by morning! If he is a god, let him plead for himself, because his altar has been torn down!" – (Judges 6:31)

Beloved, make no mistake about this, there is a spirit behind every altar.

Christianity recognizes the spirit world and the reality of the devil and all its demons.

Every spirit is looking for a vessel to use whether that vessel is a man or woman, animal or tree. They can't operate without a ready and willing vessel.

By virtue of the ministry and the grace of God, one has at various times and ways encounter evil altars for their destruction.

There is nothing to gain intimidating or deceiving you. There is something behind that altar in your father's house and that something is a spirit.

That is what you must address if you will make head way in faith and life.

The bible tells us in Ephesians six and verse twelve,

> ***"For we do not wrestle against flesh and blood, but against principalities, against powers, against rulers of the darkness of this age, against spiritual hosts of wickedness in the heavenly places" – (Ephesians 6:12)***

Understand that this very scripture was written to the Ephesians church. It was a response to informed, equipped and encouraged them to stand strong in the faith. It means something was not right with them at the time and they needed to know what it was and fight to overcome it.

Then this letter was written to point them to the reality of the spiritual warfare.

Apart from the physical realm of life there is also the spiritual realm. And the earlier you realize that the spiritual is real and that it is the spiritual that control the physical, the better for you.

The point is this; don't just pull down the physical altar or shrine, deal with the power behind the altar.

Why?

Your deliverance is incomplete until you deal with the power behind the evil altar.

Jesus said to cast out the evil spirit. So pull down the physical altar and be sure the evil spirit behind the altar is cast out and sent away.

Once the evil altar is destroyed, a new altar must be raised for the lord. This is one way to keep the evil spirit away.

Don't forget, altar is a place of sacrifice and worship. When an altar is raised to God, it brings God's presence and blessing to bear upon the land and the people. It also serves as a memorial of an existing covenant.

Both Gideon and Elijah had to raise a new altar to the Lord in place of the evil altar. You have to do the same in your family to bring divine presence and blessing into your father's house.

In order to keep your deliverance, you and your family must dedicate yourselves to worship and serve the lord in spirit and truth.

Moses was careful to follow through every instruction He received from the Lord and one of such instruction was to keep alive the lamp and fire on the altar.

Today, it means a life of non- stop worship and service to the Lord God almighty.

Jesus was very clear about this in the book of Mathew.

"When an unclean spirit goes out of a man, he goes through dry places, seeking rest, and finds none.

Then he says, I will return to my house from which I came.' And when he comes, he finds it empty, swept, and put in order.

***Then he goes and takes with him seven other spirits more wicked than himself, and they entered and dwell there; and the last case of that man is worse than the first. So shall it also be with this wicked generation."* – (Mathew 12:43-45)**

What does the scripture mean by empty, swept and put in order?

It means to keep the door open for demon spirits to return. It means to repeat the same mistakes that brought them in the first time.

As they always say, 'You can't eat your cake and have it."

If you became lose and relaxed because you got deliverance and prosperity, you risk another attack. And may God help you if you survived it.

The devil is a business man; he never gives up on his tactics and determination to get men down the way of destruction.

You must wise up to resist him by continuous worship and service to God. I mean you must be zealous for the lord and in the lord service.

Joshua declared, I and my family shall serve the lord God of Israel.

"Now therefore, fear the lord, serve Him in sincerity and in truth, and put away the gods which your fathers served on the other side of the river and in Egypt. Serve the Lord!

And if it seems evil to you to serve the Lord, choose for yourselves this day whom you will serve, whether the gods of which your fathers served that were on

the other side of the river, or the gods of the Amorites, in whose land you dwell. But as for me and my house, we will serve the Lord." – (Joshua 24:14, 15)

You see, you must be clear and firm in your resolve to worship and serve the Lord.

As a family, not every one may agree to follow you in this kind of situation. Certainly some will be for and others against but you must fight for your head where that is the case.

Don't wait for everyone to be on the same page with you. But if you think you have the time why not, if not. Do your utmost best to carry every one along.

If you cannot get everyone to follow this program, you can fight to save your head. But it may means there is limit to what you can and will do.

Now, having done what ought to be done, expect your miracle. Your change must come.

"Therefore do not cast away your confidence which has a great reward.

For you have need of endurance, so that after you have done the will of God, you may receive the promise." – (Hebrews 10:35, 36)

Hear me well; some family deliverance does not happen overnight. It may take a painstaking effort and repeated and consistence prayer to break the yoke. And so you really need patience endurance to get over the evil.

Everything about Christianity is about faith. It takes faith to be born again and remain a Christian. It takes faith to receive and keep your testimony.

Your family deliverance requires the same faith.

And so go ahead and start giving praise to God for the miracles of his mercies and deliverance.

Don't hesitate to give thanks.

Prayer Points

- Give thanks to God for the revelation you have received
- Rebuke every spirit of fear in the name of Jesus.
- Pray that every hidden truth that will facilitate your deliverance be revealed in the name of Jesus.
- Pray that the Lord will perfect that which concerns you and your deliverance
- Come against every spirit of error and carelessness during and after your deliverance
- Reaffirm your faith in the Lord in the name of Jesus.
- Thank the Lord because God will reward your obedience and faith with success.

Chapter 5: How To Prepare For Family Deliverance

No two families are the same. Each work of deliverance is determined by a number of factors which will include the depth of involvement in cultic activities and the faith of the people who is or are carrying out the deliverance.

No deliverance will take place without the cooperation of the people involved. Of course, two can only work together by agreement.

Getting your family together for this program will not happen by share luck. It will require a dialogue among believers in the family unless you want to undertake it alone which is also very possible.

If you get the cooperation of others, good and fine but if not carry on, the Lord will fight for you.

You can actually carry on alone but two are always better than one. If you want to do the program alone, you must be sure of your spiritual and Christian status.

There is what a child can and will do and there is also what you will need the guidance of an adult to do.

In (Acts 19:13) is the story of the seven sons of Sceva a Jewish priest who were injured by a demon possessed man.

"Then some of the itinerant Jewish exorcists took it upon themselves to call the name of the Lord Jesus over those who had evil spirits, saying, we exorcise you by the Jesus whom Paul preaches."

Also there were seven sons of Sceva, a Jewish chief priest, who did so.

"And the evil spirit answered and said, "Jesus I know, and Paul I know, but who are you?"

Then the man in whom the evil spirit was leaped on them, overpowered them, and

prevailed against them, so that they fled out of that house naked and wounded.

This became known both to all Jews and Greeks dwelling in Ephesus; and fear fell on them all and the name of the Lord Jesus was magnified." – (Acts 19:13-17)

I said it before and will not neglect to say it again if there is a need to remind you that there is a spirit behind every altar or shrine.

And if your fathers had reasons to invite them in to your family, then you cannot deny their existence and make light of their powers.

The sons of Sceva surely crossed their boundary when they attempted to free the demon possessed by the name of Jesus. They did not know or believed in the lordship of Jesus.

Of course, there are depths of knowledge and fellowship. Jesus and Paul were spiritual authority the demon understood and must obeyed but not so with the sons of Sceva.

After a careful study of your foundation, you must ascertain where you come in and where you will or may need help.

In seeking for help, remember you don't have to ignore or compromise the scriptures. Let the word of God guide you through out the program.

This is necessary because there are scriptural and unscriptural ways to do these things. Be careful too, because the fact that it works does not mean that it was God that worked it.

The Lord also warned that Satan cannot cast out Satan.

What I am saying is this; you don't need Spiritualist to carry out your family or personal deliverance.

Always have your salvation in view as you seek solution-healing, deliverance or breakthrough in life.

The scriptures admonished us to contend for the faith. In other words, do your best to defend your salvation because it will always come under attack.

In the name of finding a way out of life's many troubles some have lost their salvation trading it for material and earthly things.

The writer of the book of Proverbs told us of a way that looks bright and very promising but its end is the way of death.

The broad way is always a popular way but leads to death.

No sacrifice is too much to make for the salvation of your soul and that is most important to God than everything else.

I think that was the heart reason the three Hebrews boys were ever willing to be cast into the fiery furnace of fire in Babylon.

Even though they were thrown into that burning fire, they walked out of it all like kings because of their confidence in the God of Israel.

And so be strong in the lord and in the power of his might and you too will win. You will overcome your challenge if you will hold on to Him who alone can help you without mockery.

Our God is able and He is the God of all flesh. There is nothing impossible with Him.

Be determined to win for that is what is expected of you and that is who you are in Christ -a winner.

There is no known method of prayer that will get you out of the wood. What you must do in preparing for this program is to

Set the day(s) and time for this program.

No two foundations are the same. For some a day, two or three days are enough. For others more may be required to do the prayer. It all depends on what is on ground to deal with.

When I did mine, it took me twenty one days of fasting and prayer. It was at the end of that fasting and prayer that the ministers showed up to pray with us.

Make up your mind to pray according to the scriptures.

Daniel was set to pray but we were not told for how long. But you know that he ended up praying for three weeks.

Why was that?

The scriptures tell us the priest of Persia did hindered Angel Gabriel from delivering the answer to his prayer. Michael has to intervene before Gabriel could deliver his message to Daniel.

In praying a prayer of this magnitude, I recommend that you listen more to the Spirit guidance. No room for assumption. Yes, faith is standing on the word and the word is the greatest revelation and prophecy any one will ever had. But the same scripture tells us those who are led by the spirit are the sons of God. Both will guide you to victory and ensure a balance. Don't neglect either of them.

Be very sensitive to the Spirit's promptings.

Let your team cooperate with one another that is if you have a team to work with.

Two can only work together by agreement and so ensure there is agreement and do whatever you can to achieve it.

Get ready to sow seed of faith or give honorarium to your team of ministers after the exercise. That is a necessary sacrifice.

Let your seed be a sacrifice, something that even God will appreciate.

What you give matters and the heart with which you gave too. You know what is good for you. Do the same to others.

Be read to rededicate your life and family to God.

Remember that there is no other sacrifice for sin. The sacrifice of Jesus on the cross is sufficient for your deliverance. Beware of men who will ask you to engage in some sort of sacrifices of animals or leads you to do some undefined and unscriptural work or rituals.

Raising a new altar for yourself and family only means you dedicate or rededicate your life and family to the worship and service of God.

Prayer Points

- Pray very well that you will not compromised your salvation and faith in the Lord.
- Pray that like the three Hebrews' boys you will remain firm in your resolve to follow the Lord.
- Pray that God will expose every spirit of deception in the name of Jesus.
- Command your testimony in the name of Jesus.
- Pray that evil will not befall you in this project in the name of Jesus.
- Pray for all those that will join you or minister to you in this project that the

anointing will rest on them for your deliverance.

- Pray for provision and direction in this project in the name of Jesus.

Chapter 6: 21 Prayer Points To Undo The Evil Foundation

"Then He spoke a parable to them, that men always ought to pray and not lose heart, Saying: There was in a certain city a judge who did not fear God nor regard man. Now there was a widow in that city; and she came to him, saying, 'Get justice for me from my adversary.

And he would not for a while; but afterward he said within himself, 'Though I do not fear God nor regard man, yet because this widow troubles me I will avenge her, lest by her continual coming she weary me. Then the Lord said, Hear what the unjust judge said.

And shall God not avenge His own elect who cry out day and night to Him, though He bears long with them?

I tell you that He will avenge them speedily. Nevertheless, when the son of Man comes, will

He really find faith on the earth?" – (Luke 18:1-8)

Beloved, it takes faith to receive from God. Of a truth, faith is the currency of the Christian faith.

Let me put it this way that faith is your patience trust in the word of God. It is your righteous standing in the word irrespective of circumstantial evidence.

The concern of the Lord in that passage is whether you will trust Him long enough. Because the answer to your request will certainly come but will you wait if it tarries a little longer?

Oftentimes, we come to the altar of prayer under immense pressure with predetermined answer and timing.

And when it lingers and does not come our way, we turn to self-help or seek alternative way out of the situation.

Here is a call to persist in faith and prayer and never to give up because God is faithful. He will answer you in the name of Jesus!

But note that some deliverance may linger, that is one reason you must persist in prayer.

In this program, you must persist in prayer because your deliverance is sure but how long will it take to manifest?

Beloved it is very easy to bring down or destroy a building or foundation than raise one. Good dreams and things of life take time to materialize.

Satan will always fight silly and mad but God always prevail. You will win this fight in the name of Jesus.

Below are some suggested prayer points that will guide you in this program.

Do this program with fasting. Fasting is part and parcel of the Christian faith. But understand that your deliverance does not depend on the fast.

And so don't do a fast that will endanger your health.

- Commit your time to this program, pray your heart and let the name of God be glorified.
- Seven or twenty one day the choice is yours. Let's go.
- Give thanks to God for all His goodness to you and your father's house. Psalm136:1
- Give thanks to God for the salvation of your soul and for His anointing upon your life.
- Confess and repent of every sin of your father's house.
- Ask the lord for mercy and forgiveness in the name of Jesus
- Pray that the blood of Jesus will begin to speak mercy and sanctification for your father's house.
- Plead the blood of Jesus 3x and command every evil transaction and covenants to be destroyed in the name of Jesus. Decree that

they shall be of no effect in your life and family forever.

- Plead the blood of Jesus 3x and command and rebuke every evil altar speaking against you and your father's house in the name of Jesus.
- Plead the blood of Jesus 3x and command every evil sacrifice on the evil altar to catch fire in the name of Jesus.
- Call the name of Jesus powerfully and command the evil altar to release you and your father's house.
- Call the name of Jesus powerfully and command the evil altar to release the glory and destiny of your father's house.
- Call the name of Jesus powerfully and command the spirits and power behind the evil altar to go out of your father's house. Please call the idols by their names and command them to go.
- Call the name of Jesus and pull down the evil altar by fire in the name of Jesus.

Remove the altar and burn the token with fire in the name of Jesus.

- Plead the blood of Jesus 3x and reclaim the land and your father's house in the name of Jesus
- Decree that every curse against you and your father's house be destroyed in the name of Jesus. Dedicate yourself and family to the worship and service of the almighty God.
- Decree every unrepentant strong man in your father's house holding brief for the idols be arrested by fire in the name of Jesus.
- Decree every curse, covenant and transactions of the devil in your father's house be uprooted in Jesus name.
- Cry to God every blood and voice of vengeance crying against the land and my father's compound and people be truncated in the name of Jesus.

- Pray very well; every blood and voice of vengeance crying and speaking against you and your father's house become silence forever in Jesus name.
- Decree and declare that you and your father's house are free from every curse, covenant and transactions that were binding the family in the name of Jesus.
- Decree and declare that you recover every lost glory, honor, gifts, throne, riches and wealth that were lost to the devil in the name of Jesus.
- Give thanks to God for your deliverance and freedom in the name of Jesus.

About The Book

- Do you really care to know the root causes of your challenges in life?
- Do you know that evil or cursed foundation can ruin everything you are trying to build?
- Do you know for sure what is fighting you or what you are fighting against in life?
- Do you have problem in your life you cannot explain?
- In your experience of life, do you notice a repeat of what happened to your fathers and other family members repeating again in your life and days?

This book "How To Discover And Break Generational Curses" is a step by step prayer guide that helps you discover what exactly is fighting against you and prayers to destroy it.

You don't need to die for the sins of your father's house. And you don't have to repeat the mistakes of your fathers. Foundation has a voice. Stop them before they stop you.

The fact is, you came from a family with defined principles and rules of engagement. You need to investigate, interrogate and break free before it's too late.

Get this book and discover what you need to do and undo to end the problems associated with evil foundation in your life and family.

About The Author

Efemena Aziakpono Anthony is a husband, father and a minister of the gospel of Jesus Christ. He is the founder of Gospel Light Global mission, an emerging church and mission body in Lagos, Nigeria.

He is a product of the leadership certificate course of Word of life bible institute and obtains a diploma in theology from the Redeemed Christian Bible College.

He is called and sent to the body of Christ as an apostle, prophet and teacher.

This is one of his contribution to the body of Christ in particular and humanity in general from his many years of experience of life and ministry to point the way forward for those coming behind and has been a blessing in his own sphere of influence.

He presently resides in Lagos where he has been serving in the Lord's vineyard.

Glory be to God.

Made in the USA
Columbia, SC
15 March 2025